SPORTS BIOGRAPHIES

COCO GAUFF

KENNY ABDO

Fly!

An Imprint of Abdo Zoom

abdobooks.com

abdobooks.com

Published by Abdo Zoom, a division of ABDO, P.O. Box 398166, Minneapolis, Minnesota 55439. Copyright © 2021 by Abdo Consulting Group, Inc. International copyrights reserved in all countries. No part of this book may be reproduced in any form without written permission from the publisher. Fly!™ is a trademark and logo of Abdo Zoom.

Printed in the United States of America, North Mankato, Minnesota.
052020
092020

THIS BOOK CONTAINS RECYCLED MATERIALS

Photo Credits: Alamy, AP Images, Icon Sportswire, iStock, newscom, Shutterstock
Production Contributors: Kenny Abdo, Jennie Forsberg, Grace Hansen
Design Contributors: Dorothy Toth, Neil Klinepier

Library of Congress Control Number: 2019956161

Publisher's Cataloging-in-Publication Data

Names: Abdo, Kenny, author.
Title: Coco Gauff / by Kenny Abdo
Description: Minneapolis, Minnesota : Abdo Zoom, 2021 | Series: Sports biographies | Includes online resources and index.
Identifiers: ISBN 9781098221379 (lib. bdg.) | ISBN 9781098222352 (ebook) | ISBN 9781098222840 (Read-to-Me ebook)
Subjects: LCSH: Professional athletes--United States--Biography--Juvenile literature. | Women tennis players-Biography--Juvenile literature. | African American women tennis players--Biography--Juvenile literature. | Teenage athletes--Biography-Juvenile literature.
Classification: DDC 796.342092 [B]--dc23

TABLE OF CONTENTS

COCO GAUFF

Coco Gauff is a **premier** tennis player who has served up many losses to her fierce opponents.

Although young in age, Gauff has the impressive track record of a seasoned champion.

EARLY YEARS

Cori "Coco" Gauff was born in Delray Beach, Florida, in 2004. She was raised in Atlanta, Georgia.

Gauff and her family moved from Georgia to Florida when she was seven. They moved so she could train year-round in tennis, her passion.

In 2012, Gauff won the **Little Mo** 8-under Nationals. At 10, she won the USTA (United States Tennis Association) National Clay Court 12-under **title**.

GOING PRO

Gauff was selected to be trained by Patrick Mouratoglou at just 11 years old. Mouratoglou trained Serena and Venus Williams, two of Gauff's idols.

All of the training paid off in 2018. Gauff won her first Junior Grand Slam **title**. It was at the Roland Garros Junior French **Championships** in France!

Gauff won the prestigious
Orange Bowl International Tennis
Championships later that year.
She defeated her **rival** from China,
Qinwen Zheng.

In 2019, Gauff made history at her Grand Slam **debut** at Wimbledon. She beat Venus Williams in a **straight-sets** victory.

0.17

POINTS

0

3 15

Gauff continued her amazing **streak** in Linz, Austria. She beat Jelena Ostapenko in the Upper Austria Ladies Open in 2019.

LEGACY

Gauff's victory in Linz made her the youngest woman to win a WTA (Women's Tennis Association) **title**. She was also the youngest finalist in the girls' singles event at the US Open.

Gauff played in the very first Baha Mar Cup. It raised more than $100,000 for those affected by Hurricane Dorian.

GLOSSARY

championship – a game held to find a first-place winner.

debut – a first appearance.

Little Mo – refers to the tennis player Maureen Connolly. She was the first woman to win a Grand Slam. Little Mo tournaments are held each year.

premier – first in position. Always leading.

rival – a person who is competing for the same goal as another.

straight-sets – achieved in the minimal possible number of sets.

streak – a period of continual wins.

title – a first-place position in a contest.

ONLINE RESOURCES

Booklinks
NONFICTION NETWORK
FREE! ONLINE NONFICTION RESOURCES

To learn more about Coco Gauff, please visit **abdobooklinks.com** or scan this QR code. These links are routinely monitored and updated to provide the most current information available.

INDEX